RUGGER BUGGER MAN

"Rugby is like war;
easy to start, difficult to
stop...and impossible to
forget"

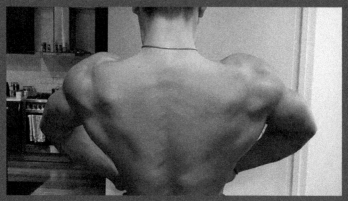

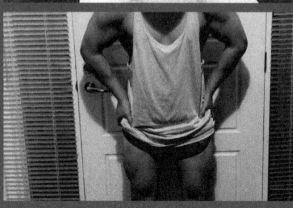

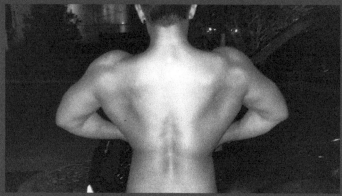

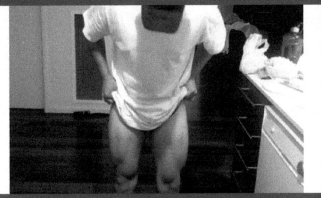

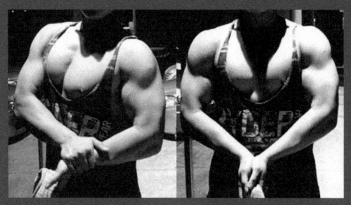

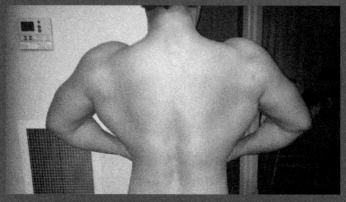

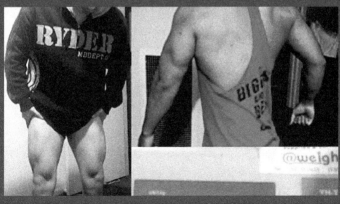

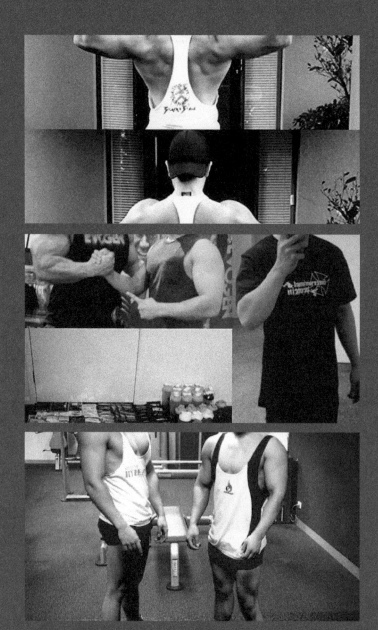

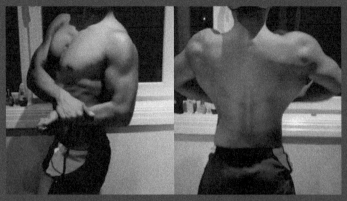

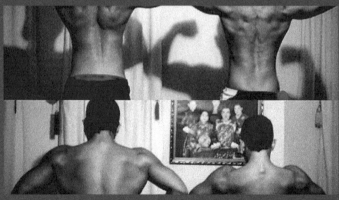

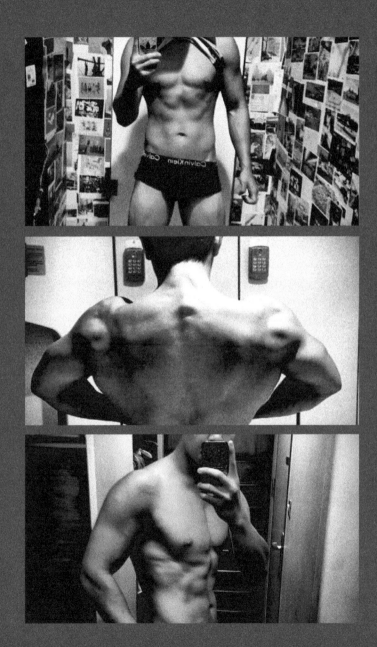

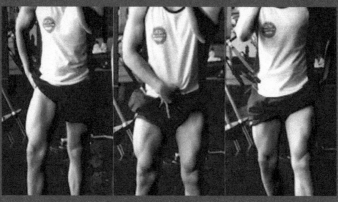

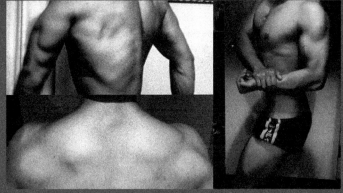

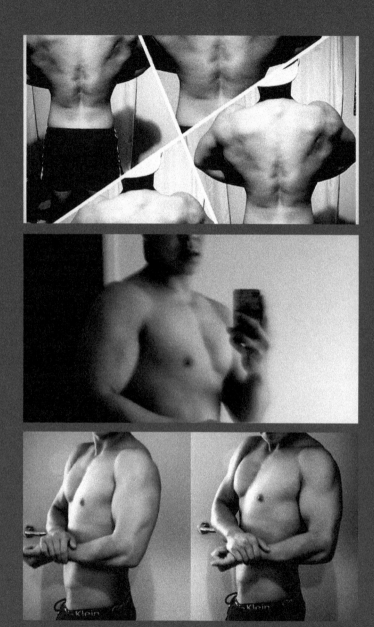

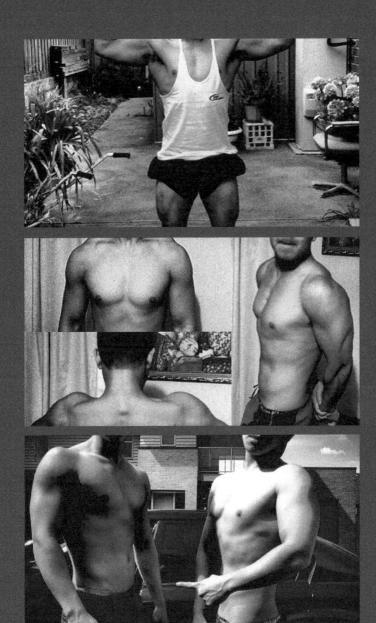

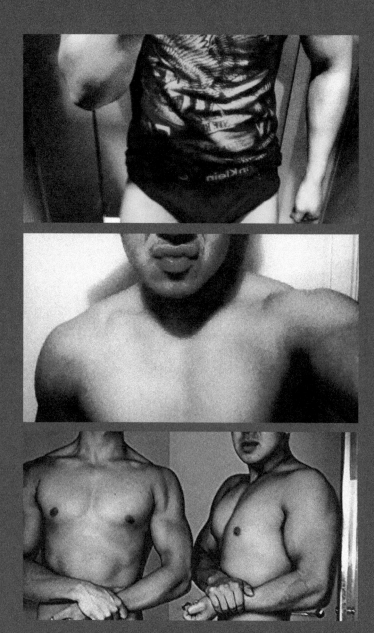

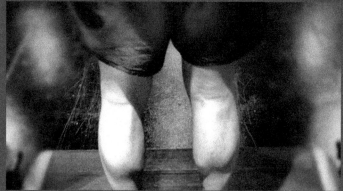

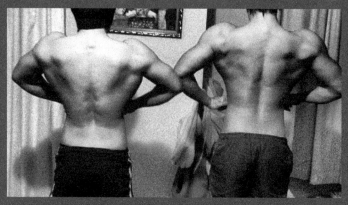

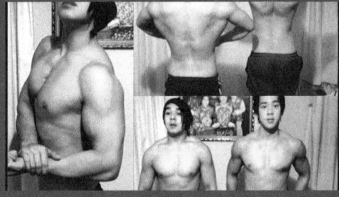

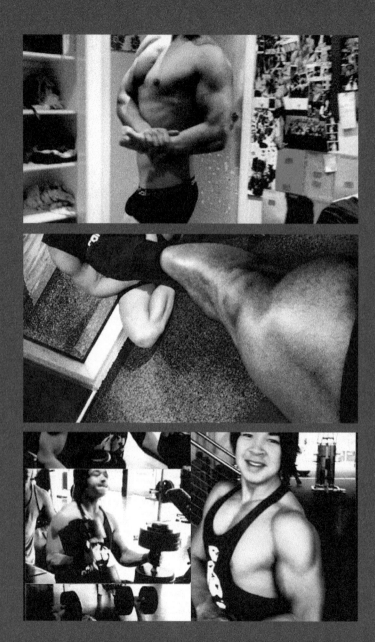

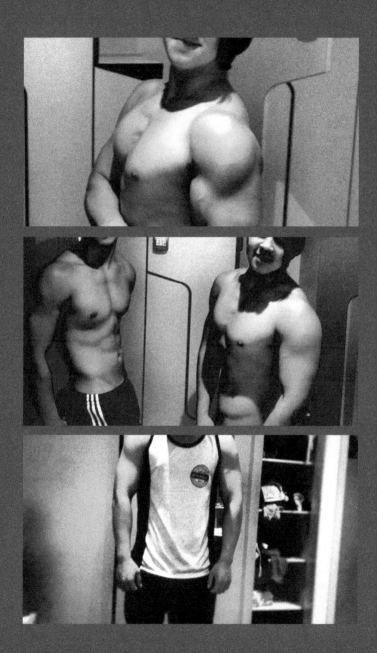

CPSIA information can be obtained
at www.ICGtesting.com
Printed in the USA
BVHW021957280719
554531BV00010B/244/P

9 780464 104650